T0065568

Romantic and Sexual Satisfaction in Marriage

REV. COL. ADENIRAN GBOLAGADE JACOB

authorHOUSE®

AuthorHouse™ UK
1663 Liberty Drive
Bloomington, IN 47403 USA
www.authorhouse.co.uk
Phone: 0800.197.4150

Published by AuthorHouse 06/21/2016

ISBN: 978-1-5246-3530-5 (sc)
ISBN: 978-1-5246-3529-9 (e)

Library of Congress Control Number: 2016908902

Print information available on the last page.

This book is printed on acid-free paper.

Scripture quotations marked NIV are taken from the Holy Bible, New International Version, copyright ©1973, 1978, 1984 by International Bible Society. Used by permission of Zondervan. All rights reserved.

This book is dedicated to the glory of God for all homes.

CONTENTS

ACKNOWLEDGEMENTS

We acknowledge the help of the Holy Spirit in writing this book. We are indebted to our children, Joshua, Samuel, Joseph, and Daniel, for their understanding and encouragement.

We also acknowledge the typing of Mrs Okunade and Pastor Oluyole's secretary, who did the initial typing under tight schedule. We appreciate all participants in our couples seminars, workshops, and counselling, whose questions prompted us to write this book for the benefit of humanity.

I recommend this book for every genuine seeker of God's will in marriage. This book in your hand is a pathfinder, is a book of wisdom and is a key that will open the door of an un-regrettable marital relationship. Why did I say this? Because it teaches you how to discover the right person to marry, how to become the right person yourself; because marriage may be made in heaven but maintenance must be done on earth. This book equally teaches you how to recognize the voice of God, different ways by which God talks to people, the secret of a successful courtship and many more. That is why is a must read for all singles whose desire is to seek the will of God in marriage and how to have a successful marital life. Congratulations! If these are your needs; you don't need to search any further because the answer is already in your hands through this book.

Pastor Paul D. Oluyole
Freedom Gate Int'l Christian Centre
Author and Motivational Speaker

A WORD OF WELCOME

The situation of parental failure due to failure of marriage is the main motivation for this write-up. The most neglected root cause of failure in marriage is the sexual relationship in marriage. This book has attempted to examine and discuss the vitality of a healthy sexual relationship as a panacea for the collapse of marriages as a result of sexual matters.

Multiple social events emanating from irresponsible sexual relationships in marriages have compounded our sociocultural lives. The situation is so precarious that most youths have never even witnessed a good marital relationship for them to emulate. This is due to the long-term negligence of good virtues and the sanctity of marriage. We join forces with other discerning authors on the subject of sexual relationships in marriages, and to bridge the gap of knowledge of couples as to how best to conduct their sexual relationships, with the view to building a strong, lasting marriage. This book is geared towards having practical reference material for all who want a blissful marriage with high resistance to wrong values that are prevalent in society. This book itself is not exhaustive in all issues destroying marriages and homes. However, it brings to the foreground the pivotal issue of sexual relationships, which affect the cohesion of marriages.

As you read, the Holy Spirit will help you to find relevant help, support, instruction, and information, which will help heal your homes and marriages.

God bless you.

INTRODUCTION

Notwithstanding the fact that God established marriages, different people have different perspectives on what marriage is. To many it is a social contract between a man and woman from a legal perspective. Others see marriage from a traditional point of view, whereby upon maturity tradition requires young men and women to start their lives together.

There are other perspectives of what marriage is to many people, however drawing from the fact that God established the marriage institution, there is a need to put into proper perspective what marriage is as originally planned and ordained by Him. "God wants you to have a marriage full of love and passion." These are the words of Dr Willard F. Harley Junior, author of *His Needs, Her Needs*.

What Is Marriage?

"Marriage is God's vision for a man and woman to live together their lives for God's mission to be fulfilled – helping each other" (Gen. 2:18–25). Marriage is a highly spiritual arrangement which is lived out in flesh among many other people who have direct and indirect influences on the marriage. This probably explains why marriages are grossly misunderstood and mismanaged. The parties involved in a marriage (man and woman) must revere God for meaningful and successful marriage. "Marriage is honourable among all, and the bed undefiled" (Heb. 13:4, KJV). This scripture is the peak of God's interest in the purity of marriage and sexual relationships in marriage.

This book is divinely placed in your hands to equip you for the journey of life in marriage using God's way, in order to have a successful and happy marriage. For a maximum positive impact in your marriage, you are encouraged to read this book jointly with your spouse, or you should create time to discuss topical issues raised in this book – in person with your spouse, not through electronic media!

Chapter 1

FOUNDATION OF A SUCCESSFUL AND ROMANTIC MARRIAGE

A lot of activities are involved in marriage, from physical to spiritual. Bearing this truth in mind, the nature of a marriage that will be successful will require both unilateral and mutual reasoning by the husband and wife in order to make the lifetime journey of marriage a success. These fundamental, foundational commitments to the success of the marriage is a major ingredient for a successful marriage. Why must this be? A husband and wife must come to a level of understanding of this commitment. When the foundation for good collapses, what can good people do? (See Ps. 11:3, WCV.) It is the foundation that determines outcome when challenges come.

Josh D. McDowell, in his article "Is the Bible Sexually Oppressive?", has this to say about sex from God's perspective. "God is pro-sex! He invented sex and thinks is beautiful when enjoyed within the correct frame work." Proverbs tells us, "Take pleasure in the wife of your youth …

let her breast always satisfy you; be lost in her love forever" (Prov. 5:18–19). The context here is speaking of sex within the parameters of a lifelong marriage commitment (i.e., "the wife of your youth"). Another example of God's perspective on sex is the Song of Songs, an Old Testament book that uses the beauty of sexual experience to express one's spiritual experience.

A successful marriage needs God's perspective of sexual relationship. Referring to the wife of your youth in Proverbs 5:18–19 presupposes that even at advanced ages, married couples are obliged to enjoy and be satisfied with their physique in a romantic sense. In other words, they should both appreciate their God-given bodies as it ages. It is interesting to note that breastfeeding of the children is not the sole purpose for why God created breasts; they are also for the husband to enjoy, as supported by this scripture. The firmness of the breast does not reduce the satisfaction a husband gets from the wife's breast at anytime and at any stage of the marriage. The general area of problem in this respect is a psychological belief and feeling by both husband and wife. This is seen apparently in the psychological withdrawal of most wives after breastfeeding children; they no longer see their breasts as instruments of sexual satisfaction for their husbands. For example, before most ladies get married, they jealously take care of their breasts, avoiding touches and viewing from people other than their lovers. This attitude generally communicates affection, love, and sexuality to their would-be husbands at that stage of the relationship.

It must be noted, however, that the attitude of some young mothers not breastfeeding their babies long out of a fear of breast flaccidity is unhealthy and ungodly. The breast milk is made with enough minerals and water for the breastfeeding of babies. We join the advocates of baby-friendly breastfeeding, which is exclusive breastfeeding of babies for a minimum for at least six months. This helps the baby's immunity against diseases.

We are pleased to share with you that our four boys were breastfed for fourteen months each. That is a cumulative breastfeeding of fifty-six months, and this has not removed the satisfaction we enjoy in our sexual relationship to date, till death do us part!

It is interesting to note that one of our boys was recognized in Lagos State, Nigeria, as the best breastfed baby of 2002, which is an annual award organized during World Breastfeeding Week.

Husbands need to understand that their wives' breasts are created by God to be satisfying in a sexual relationship on equal terms, whether the breasts are firm or flat. This is very important in a sexual relationship. It is also important to note that this is an area of a high level of seduction for married men, who don't understand this fact. Such men are easily seduced by younger ladies whose breasts are pointed and firm. In most cases, some seducers use this as a means of luring married men out of their marriages. This may eventually lead to extramarital affairs, which are inimical to successful marriages. This situation reinforces the need for couples to get sexually romantic and to fend off their marriages from seducers.

The main aim of this book is to get married couples to go back to the drawing board and revitalize their sexual attraction with the same purpose of making their marriages strong, fruitful, enjoyable, blissful, and romantic again, creating continuous romantic and sexual satisfaction in the marriage.

Here are some potential factors in a marriage.

- The couples have an age disparity.

> *Marriage is designed to be a life time relationship.*

- The couples have different backgrounds and upbringings.

- There are different intellectual capacities due to educational qualifications and diverging fields of study.

- The couples may have different traditions and cultures.

- The couples may have different social exposure.

- The couples may have come from different faiths.

Most times these natural facts of life are either disregarded or downplayed. When it comes to issues of marriage, these are usually the issues that make a marriage fail. Because of these reasons and more, no two marriages are the same.

Marriage is designed to be a lifetime relationship. It is therefore necessary for husbands and wives to be ready to learn and teach one another. That way they can survive the challenges mentioned above. There is no gainsaying that the listed factors are enough to occupy a husband and wife for a lifetime based on their resolved commitment to one another. That is why people say marriage is a continuous overlooking of faults. It is a learning institution, and there is no level of perfection. This imperfection is the reason why marriages of one year may have problems. Marriages of ten years or even thirty years have their problems.

Things Couples Must Always Bear in Mind

- **Accept each other.** Marriage is an acceptance to live together in love despite the weaknesses of one another (1 Cor. 13:1–13). Weaknesses will definitely be in everyone. If we were perfect, we should have been taken like Enoch in the Bible; we should not be on earth.

- **Mutual accountability and responsibility.** A husband and wife must be accountable to each other. As much as you want to know about your spouse, you must also give much more information, responsibility, comfort, happiness, service, and support to your spouse (Rom. 14:12; Eph. 5:21; Eph. 6: 6).

- **Conflict resolution.** Conflicts must come (Prov. 18:19). The reality of conflict cannot be wished away. The ability for resolving conflict is fundamental for a successful marriage.

- **God must rule in your home.** Fear of God, love of God, obedience to the word of God, and service of God are sure means by which a marriage can have a solid foundation. "Choose ye this day whom you will serve, as for me and my house we will serve the Lord" (Josh. 1:9).

Notes

The ability for conflict resolution by the couple is fundamental for a successful marriage.

Chapter 2

MARITAL BONDING

Bonding together for husband and wife entails social adjustments in character, interests, and use of time and resources to make one another the object of attraction.

"Therefore a man shall leave his father and mother and cling to his wife" (Gen 2:24, KJV). This Bible reference reveals the heart of God for a husband and wife becoming one through bonding, orchestrated by conscious and deliberate disengagement from activities capable of impeding them from bonding together as husband and wife. In other words, if God expects a man to leave his parents, where he has spent a minimum of two decades of his life, to concentrate on and give priority to his wife, bonding together as husband and wife

It is important to stress that activities that promotes bonding between husband and wife should not be limited to early stage of marriage love euphoria. It must be understood to be a continuous thing throughout life time of that relationship.

is therefore a must for a romantic and successful marriage.

The process of heart-to-heart bonding between husband and wife requires determination and agreeable activities that become a substitute for the object of attention. These activities will gradually replace previous activities that had gained their attention prior to marriage. Some examples of such activities could be time spent alone with friends on vacation, visiting relatives, and recreation. These previous activities could be harmonized now to be joint activities with your spouse, but some of these activities have to be forgotten.

Bonding together for husband and wife entails social adjustments in character, interests, and use of time and resources to make one another the object of attraction.

The primary objective of bonding for husband and wife is to elicit, promote, facilitate, and ensure opportunities for the demonstration of love for one another. In other words, bonding together is jointly seeking and creating opportunities that will be the platform for which both husband and wife can appreciate their innermost affectionate feelings for one another. The adjustment required for bonding could mean learning a new thing together or playing a particular game together, which will offer a good opportunity to bond together. Learning to play the same set of games in another way or form can offer a more interesting means of bonding together. Outdoor activities such as visits to parks, wedding ceremonies, social programmes, and visiting work places is a proven, reliable way of bonding. Bonding together is a creative means of working together towards a romantic and successful marriage. Both husband and wife have to work hard to create these opportunities for bonding together.

The use of God-given talents and spiritual gifts could be exploited by the couple to promote their bonding. Such talents and gifts could be singing, dancing, acting, organizing, or teaching others. The art of conscious involvement in activities between husband and wife tends to completely eliminate gaps that existed between both of them prior to marriage. Gaps of communication, gaps due to inferiority and superiority complexes, and other imaginable gaps are narrowed or completely eliminated, thereby moving the couple towards becoming one individual, as expected by God. It is important to stress that activities that promote bonding between husband and wife should not be limited to the early stage of marriage's love euphoria. It must be understood to be a continuous thing throughout the lifetime of that relationship. This understanding will help when children come into the marriage. Activities such as eating, bathing, sleeping together, and understanding the need for bonding together will replace the ones that have been displaced when they started raising their children. Some of the activities that will replace former activities include reading books aloud together, watching movies, and playing indoor games after the children have been put to bed. The bonding activities in a marriage are dynamic because changes occur in the family in terms of

> *Marriage is the bonding of two unbeatable teams. Marriage is good and is meant to be enjoyed and not endured.*

ageing, children maturity, and communal responsibility.

Activities for bonding have to revolve around these changes. Some other forms of bonding at this stage include family retreats, vacations, volunteering, involvement in seminars, mutual support activities, and the like. A biblical example is Isaac and Rebecca sporting together, which made Abimelech know that they were husband and wife (Gen. 26:8–9).

Concerning marital bonding, a story is told of the couple Disraeli and Mary Anne. Disraeli's marriage was one of the most glowing successes in matrimony. The rich widow whom Disraeli chose was neither young nor beautiful, with a provoking display of illiteracy and historical blunders. But she was genius at the most important thing in marriage: the art of handling men. She did not attempt to set up her riches against Disraeli. Whenever he came home bored and exhausted after an afternoon of matching report with witty duchesses, Mary Anne's frivolous pattern permitted him to relax. To his increasing delight, home was a place where he could ease into his mental slippers and bask in the warmth of Mary Anne's adoration. Those hours he spent at home with his ageing wife were the happiest of his life.

> *Stop complaining, stop finding faults, and start living the change you expect of your spouse; see what will happen.*

She was his helpmate, his confidant, his advisor. Every night, he hurried home from the House of Commons to tell her the day's news. Whatever he undertook, Mary believed he could not fail. For thirty years, Mary Anne lived for Disraeli and for him alone. She valued her wealth only because it made his life easier, and in return she was a heroine. No matter how silly or scatterbrained she might appear in public, he never criticized her. He never uttered a word of reproach, and if anyone dared ridicule her, he sprang to her defence with ferocious loyalty.

Mary Anne wasn't perfect, yet for three decades she never got tired of talking, praising, and admiring her husband. Disraeli stated, "We have been married thirty years, and I have never been bored by her." Yet some people thought that because Mary Anne didn't know history, she must be stupid. Disraeli never made it any secret that Mary Anne was the most important thing in his life.

Mary Anne said to her friends, "Thanks to his kindness, my life was been simple, with one long scene of happiness." Between them, they had a little joke. "You know," Disraeli would say, "I only married you for your money." Mary Anne would smile and say, "Yes, but if you had to do it over again, you would marry for love, wouldn't you?"

Marriage is a bond of two people to create an unbeatable team. Marriage is good and is to be enjoyed, not endured.

Keys to Marital Bonding

For marital bonding to occur, the following keys should be looked at.

Key 1: Acceptance. Don't try to change your spouse – learn to accept him or her. If you try to change your spouse, both of you will end up frustrated. When you accept your spouse the way he or she is, then the person will end up becoming better than what you expected. Acceptance is the key to improvement and marital intimacy. Acceptance is the proof of love. Stop complaining, stop finding faults, and start living the change you expect of your spouse; see what will happen.

Key 2: **Be your spouse's best friend.** Friendship requires commitment. Friends are those wonderful people who know all about you and still like you; they love you for who you are. Friends are those wonderful people who come in at your dark moment, when everyone else is leaving. If you want to make the best of your marriage, make your spouse your closest friend. Dr Berry, the Washington D.C. clinical psychologist, says, "In order to be happy, couples must respect each other and treat their spouse as their best friend.… The most rewarding marriages are those in which the partners not only love each other, but genuinely like each other and ensure a close friendship with each other."

Key 3: **Talk.** Talk and express your feelings to your mate. Good communication is a boost to any relationship, and those couples with the most loving and harmonious relationships seem to have no problem talking to each other about anything and everything. If there are conflicts, talk them out with your mate.

A leading marriage counsellor says that at least half of all divorces result from communication gaps between spouses. A happy and intimate marriage demands a lot of talking. Talk, talk, talk about aspirations, hopes, joys, fears, and sorrows.

Key 4: Develop sexual compatibility. Sexual compatibility cements marriage relationship and reduces marital tension. It also destroys marital unfaithfulness and improves marital relationship. Dr Hamilton said, "To say that most marriage frictions does not find its source in sexual maladjustment. At any rate, the frictions which arise from other difficulties would be ignored in many cases if the sexual relationships were satisfactory." Dr Butterfields said, "Sex is but one of the many satisfactions in married life, unless this relationship is right, nothing else can be right." Make your sexual relationship right by talking about your sex life with your spouse. Make it interesting and garnish it with hot romance, kissing, foreplay, and touching every sensitive part of your spouse to help him or her enjoy sex.

Key 5: Patience. Patience is like a pill that has the capacity to build and repair a marital relationship and prevent it from breaking down. Unforgiveness, anger, bitterness, and depression destroy intimacy and sexual desire. Patience means the ability to endure delay, pain, and trials quietly and without complaining. The great antidote against anger, unforgiveness, and bitterness is patience. Patience is the mark of maturity and the key to marital bonding, peace, and happiness.

Key 6: Quality time. Good marital relationships require the seed of time. Raising great kids requires the seed of time. Let the time spent with your spouse be a rewarding time. Give him or her attention and play together. Shop together, relax together, eat together, watch movies together, pray together, and exercise together. Giving your spouse full, qualitative attention is the key to marital bonding. Your spouse deserves your time.

Key 7: Listen, listen, listen. Try to wait until the other person finishes before putting in your points or talking about your day. Listen to make sense out of what your spouse have to say before presenting your own. Talk less and listen more – that is why God gave us two ears and one mouth. Women love men who listen, men love women who listen, and children love parents who listen to them. The world is looking for listeners, because we have too many talkers. Listening shows you care.

Key 8: Maintain your attractive appearance. Appearance is power. Simply because you have gotten your spouse to the altar is no excuse to let yourself go. Don't ignore your appearance. Yes, he is only your husband, and she's only your wife, but he or she deserves the very best you have to offer. Keep your hair looking neat and clean. Keep your nails trimmed. Exercise to shed those unwanted pounds and stay healthy. Never let your spouse forget how beautiful or handsome you are. This is another key to marital bonding and sexuality.

Key 9: Respect your partner as an individual. Yes, he or she is your spouse, but first he or she is a human being with needs, interest, dreams, and desires that may differ from your own. In the best of marriages, spouses support each other's goals, stimulate their partners' growth, and boost their confidence. Don't suffocate your mate. Instead, give him or her freedom to grow and develop as an individual. The ultimate secret to a happy marriage rests on love, trust, and striking a balance between personal needs and relationship needs. Respecting your spouse's opinions, dreams, and differences are the keys to marital bonding.

Key 10: Show love. Love is not passive but active. If you love your wife or husband, then show it. Express it in the language he or she can understand. Love is not love until it is expressed. Love makes one give without expecting, covers a multitude of offences, and is the strongest force in the universe. Love will never make one accept evil reports about one's spouse. You cannot give love and not receive love in return. The best way to be your spouse's best friend is to show him or her that you really care and that you are in love. Remember, you cannot have sexual satisfaction without bonding, but it is good to have both sexual satisfaction and marital bonding.

Other Keys to Bonding and Romantic Marriage

Keep the candles of romance burning brightly in your marriage. The following list is culled from *10 Principles of Children Leadership* by Bill Knew.

- Give a smile to your partner freely, regularly, and lovingly.

- Give words of praise. Appreciate your partner for his or her efforts, commitments, love, and hard work.

- Give words of encouragement in the areas in which your mate may it difficult or even monotonous.

- Give a small love note, text message, or card.

- Give comfort when your lover needs your arms to reassure him or her.

- Give a small gift regularly, just to keep the message coming through loudly and clearly: "You're special."

- Give your energy to the task. which will brighten your partner's work.

- Give and affirming your love verbally and by tender touch. Keep saying to each other. "I love you."

Henry Fernandez wrote that in 1977, authors and researchers Nick Stinneth and John Defrain launched a study to determine keys that lead to strong families. Families were interviewed from diverse backgrounds and ethnicities. They found that strongest families shared these six key characteristics. We need to inculcate them into our families in order to have strong marital bonds and strong bonds with our children.

1. Family members enjoyed spending time together.
2. Family members were committed to each other.
3. Family members had good communication with each other.
4. Family members openly expressed their love and appreciated each other.
5. Family members had a spiritual commitment.
6. Family members maintained cohesive, close relationships with one another in crisis situations.

Notes

_____

_____

_____

_____

_____

_____

_____

_____

_____

_____

Chapter 3

ERRORS, FACTS, AND CHALLENGES OF MARRIAGE

> *The point of clarification here is that for married couples living together, the period of fasting must not be equal to a sexual relationship holiday, especially when both are not involved in fasting.*

There are common errors in dealing with sex in marriage. To start with, there is a need to review some common mistakes on sexual matters in marriage. Some of these errors are as follows.

- **Mistaking sex in marriage as a form of duty.** Some believe that sex is a duty which spouses must do. This perception leads to sexual tension in marriage. Sexual intercourse in marriage ought to be of a high sense of responsibility rather than duty. This means that the husband and wife should have high sense of being responsible for the sexual satisfaction of their spouses; it is a better perception than seeing it as a duty. If this responsibility is accepted by both spouses, they will think and plan on how best to satisfy each other sexually. This helps remove the error of manipulating each other in sex denial.

- **Lacking a desire to seek knowledge about sex.**
  This is a mistake that is common among couples, whereby they do not see any reason to acquire knowledge about sex matters. Every couple at any stage of the marriage should seek relevant knowledge about their sexual

  > *The golden rule here is that couples should never shy away from seeking knowledge or help when they are not enjoying sex in marriage.*

  responsibilities to one another. The carried-over knowledge about sex before marriage cannot last or endure to guarantee a satisfying sexual relationship for a lifetime relationship. Attending couples seminars, workshops, and talks where sex is discussed extensively will help couples. Reading books on sexual matters and marriage such as this one will add great value to romantic marital life.

  > *Sex is not just the act of penetration and ejaculation. Otherwise, sex in marriage would not be different from rape or patronizing a prostitute.*

  Seeking specific issues on sexual matters is highly recommended to guarantee a romantic marriage. In addition, seek medical treatment or advice (e.g., cases of frigidity, loss of libido) to enhance good sexual satisfaction. The golden rule here is that couples should never shy away from seeking knowledge or help when they are not enjoying sex in their marriage.

- **Avoid the illusion of physical statistics.** Most couples fall into the error of using only the physical statistics of their spouses, and they easily give up hope of ever having sexual satisfaction from their spouses. For example, some men want to have a slim spouse, but when, after one or two children, she has to expand, he will no longer find her attractive or satisfying in bed, which is an error. Another man wants a moderate-sized spouse, and if his spouse can't gain weight, he gets irritated. Do we need any of these statistics to be sexually satisfied? One man's meat seems to be another man's poison, but however the statistics may be, it should not affect sexual satisfaction. This is where acceptance of responsibility comes to play, whereby no matter the physical appearance of your spouse, you accept responsibility to sexually satisfy your spouse. Acquisition of knowledge regarding what to do and how to do it cannot be overemphasized; this is where all couples need to put acquired knowledge into play.

- **Abstinence from sex during fasting.** Where couples need to fast either for health reason or spiritual reason, total abstinence from sexual intercourse may not improve the objective of the fasting. There are times of breaking this fast, and that break offers opportunity to resume the romantic relationship among couples. The point of clarification here is that for married couples living together, the period of fasting must not be equal to a sexual relationship holiday, especially when both are not involved in fasting. Even when both are involved in fasting, they should exploit the physical pleasure of sex at break of that fasting. It is not sinful in marriage for people to fast for spiritual reasons. Let us be clear here: just as the Bible portrays that sex in marriage is not a sin, it shouldn't be the thing that will pollute your fasting unless it's by mutual agreement. Don't cajole your spouse to agree with you; it is selfish.

> *In other words, sexual intercourse in marriage is not a casual relationship. It is an involving, intimate affair between husband and wife.*

- **Abstinence during menstrual cycle**. It is very normal for the wife to have a lack of sex appeal during menstrual flow or blood flow due to health issues (Lev. 18:19). However, this does not suppress the sexual need of the husband. Therefore, it is recommended at this period that the wife should take up the challenge of meeting the sexual urge of the husband using romantic approaches. It is important for the wife to not assume that her lack of sex interest at that time will apply to the spouse. This

> *Generally, couples do not see it worthwhile to discuss their sexual experiences. This position does not hold true because spouses can have sexual urges at different times.*

is one major way by which infidelity comes into marriage, and it can render the relationship vulnerable to collapse. Unfortunately, at times some men want to justify their sexually immoral behaviours due to this natural phenomenon. There is no justification to be immoral during menstrual flow; rather, they should have discipline at this period and should not give in to the need for sexual satisfaction at this period.

At this junction, a definition of sex in marriage is necessary in other to continue other reviews of common errors of sex in marriage. What is sexual intercourse in marriage? Sexual intercourse is being spiritually motivated, psychologically attracted, and emotionally ready for a physical, romantic relationship between husband and wife using their God-given genitals, with the view of obtaining satisfaction between them. That is, sex is not just the act of just penetration and ejaculation. Otherwise, sex in marriage would not be different from rape or patronizing a prostitute. In other words, sexual intercourse in marriage is not a casual affair; it is an involving, intimate relationship between husband and wife. It is against this background that we will continue with other errors in dealing with sex in marriage.

However, this does not suppress the sexual need of the husband. Therefore, it is recommended at this period that the wife should take up the challenge of meeting the sexual urge of the husband using romantic approaches.

• **Tiredness and busyness as an excuse for lack of sex.** Sex needs physical strength and energy, and it is therefore advisable for couples to manage their physical fitness in order to have an exciting sexual relationship. They should be conscious of not getting physically exhausted to the point that they will be sexually unprepared. Couples should plan when sex is to take place. There is no hard and fast rule – it must not be at night only, and it could be the first thing in the morning. They need to find time to give their spouses sexual satisfaction.

- **Cultural inhibition and taboos.** It is generally believed that the husband should make the first move for sexual intercourse. This is borne out of cultural beliefs and taboos, which says that it only a morally loose woman makes a demand for sex. Couples are advised to study each other's appetite for sex. "Both the man and his wife were naked yet felt no shame" (Gen. 2:25, ASB). The notion that wives are there to meet their husbands' sexual needs is not correct. Both have an urge and have the right to get sexual satisfaction.

- **Sex psychology in marriage.** Phobias for sex can be a result of past experiences, distrust, and all other states of mind. Issues can lead to sexual withdrawal in marriage because sex in marriage involves psychological readiness and fitness. Efforts should be made by the couple to remove all forms of psychological problems in order for them to have enjoyable sexual intercourse. Fears of debt, loss of job, having children, and more have to be properly managed.

- **Discussion on sexual intercourse.** Generally, couples do not see it worthwhile to discuss their sexual intercourse experiences. This is a serious error because sexual experiences

Generally, couples do not see it worthwhile to discuss their sexual experiences. This position does not hold true because either spouse can have sexual urges at different times.

differ at different times, even with the same couple. A robust discussion before, during, and after sexual intercourse will not only promote bonding them together, but it will also help their trust for one another on sex-related matters. In addition to having optimal satisfaction, such discussions should focus on likes, dislikes, and anticipation for the next time for sex. Instead of couples

Notwithstanding all these, marriage solidly remains an exclusive affair for mature men and women going by the authorship of marriage, which is God Himself.

discussing other issues that do not add value to their relationships, they should focus on discussing these things.

Some Facts about Marriage

- **Marriage is a holy institution established by**

The issue of sexual immorality must be avoided and guarded against for a marriage to be romantic and successful.

God. This is a widely accepted opinion by people of all races across the world, but the variances come from individuals' understanding of God's will in marriage. This explains why some people could marry more than one husband or wife, divorce at will, and remarry at will. This book pitches tent with Christian beliefs. The holiness of marriage is based on the principles and teachings of the Bible. Therefore, the issue of sexual immorality must be avoided and guarded against in order for a marriage to be romantic and successful. The reliability of the teaching of Holy Spirit must be adhered to and embraced by the couple to preserve their marriage.

- **Jesus Christ must be invited and involved in a marriage.** The story of Jesus being invited to the wedding in Cana of Galilee clearly shows the need for couples to invite Christ into their marriages. When the bridegroom had a problem of shortage, he asked Jesus to help, and Jesus offered better help then they'd ever had (John 2:7–8). That means Jesus must be invited and present in a home for Him to be called upon when crises show up. He can make a marriage continually romantic and successful. This is an opportunity for couples reading this book to invite Jesus into their lives and ask Him to lift their burdens and to make their marriage romantic, blissful, and successful.

- **Marriage is a union between man and woman only.** Globalization, civilization, and sermonization about human rights has grossly distorted the original landscape of the marriage institution. In societies today, gays, lesbians, same-sex marriage, marriage to animals (Lev. 18:23), and marriage to the dead are practiced in parts of the world, and they have enjoyed tremendous legal support and publicity in government circles and even among some Christian denominations. Notwithstanding all these, marriage solidly remains an exclusive affair for a mature man and woman when going by the authorship of marriage, which is God Himself (Gen. 2:18). Human rights advocacy and the legal system does not validate marriage; it only gives room for perversion to the original purpose, mission, and vision of marriage.

- **Marriage is a lifetime journey.** For as long as husband and wife agree to live together in matrimony, that relationship is supposed to last for as long as both of them are alive. Ageing conditions, failing health conditions, shortage of resources (e.g., money, work, business), and others are not grounds for setting aside the agreement to be husband and wife. Compatibility is what the marriage relationship ought to focus attention on for a lifetime, not emphasizing any incompatibility between husband and wife. God detests and disapproves of any form of divorce between husband and wife

The more the two of you adjust, the better marriage you will have, and you'll enjoy your sexual relationship.

(1 Cor. 7:10–11). Therefore the husband and wife should work it out and dwell on issues that unite them, rather than focusing on issues that pull them apart. It is important to note that marriage is a journey of no divorce, no separation, no surrender, and no retreat. It is a journey of no return to bachelorhood or spinsterhood (Matt. 19:3–10), or else it will leave a scar that cannot be forgotten.

- **Coping with imperfection in marriage.** Human beings are subject to flaws and imperfections, be they related to work, ministry, or home life. Marriage is not an exception when it comes to flaws and imperfection.

  > *Marriage may not be a bed of roses, but it may be heaven on earth if we follow and obey God's principles.*

  For instance, the husband has never been a husband, and he is learning to be one. The wife has never been a wife and is learning how to be one. Even when there is a second marriage, it is still a new thing with a new person. Forgiveness as taught by Jesus Christ – that is, forgiving one another seventy times seventy in a day – will take care of imperfections not only in other issues in daily living but also in marriage (Matt. 18:21–22). Unforgiveness can hinder sexual satisfaction and make marriage not

  > *Welfare of one's spouse in terms of health, physical comfort, and recreational activities is the primary responsibility of a couple to one another.*

romantic enough. The practice of forgiving one another helps a marriage succeed. Flaws and imperfections can be in different ways, but whatever irritates you needs to be forgiven. Issues range from lack of time management, your spouse not thinking the way you think, financial mismanagement, your spouse not adhering to your advice or counsel, stubbornness, talkativeness, and wrong associations. These problems and many more need to be forgiven; moreover, your spouse is also managing *your* flaws. The more the two of you adjust, the better marriage you will have, and you'll enjoy your sexual relationship.

- **Accepting responsibilities to one another.** Marriage cannot be lived in isolation from third parties (in-laws, coworkers, neighbours). This calls for a sense of responsibility to one another regarding the interplay of interests from third parties. For instance, the responsibility for providing for one's family should not be left exclusively at the domain of in-laws or any other relative that offers to assist. The welfare of one's spouse in terms of health, physical comfort, and recreational activities is the primary responsibility of the couple to one another. For example, domestic staff are to help spouses achieve their responsibilities, but one should not leave all things to domestic staff exclusively.

- **Resources must be managed in marriage.** God blesses a home with resources, such as sharing time together and gaining additional knowledge. Finance is a basic resource that is available in marriage. Time and human resources (relations and domestic staff) should be managed in marriage. Material resources, intellectual resources (e.g., books), and spiritual-building resources available to couples must be managed. Goods and wares used to earn money in order to achieve a romance and success in marriage is daunting. Mismanaging of any of these resources can lead to tension and friction capable of messing up the marriage. Husband and wife must not necessarily be professional managers, but they must be opened to learning how best to use the resources available to them for the optimal benefit of their union.

- **God's principles must guide marriage.** Marriage is a vision of God for a mission of a husband and wife to follow the biblical principles of Jesus Christ to succeed. If this is not complied with, crises are inevitable in the marriages and are capable of sending couples to hell (Matt. 7:21). Because the will of God is not done, no matter how you do in other things, if you've disobeyed in marriage issues, it is disobedience. Marriage may not be bed of roses, but it may be heaven on earth if we follow and obey God's principles correctly (Isa. 1:19).

- **Challenges are inevitable in marriage.** All marriages must come under one challenge or another. The challenges should not consume the marriage. The husband and wife are expected to rise up against the challenges in their marriage, relying on God's principles and promises (Jer. 33:17–18). God promised David that no matter the challenges his seed would come against, it would always remain on the throne, and the priest would never fail to offer sacrifices.

- **Spouses must acknowledge and preserve each other's values.** Familiarity is a part of the husband and wife relationship. This should not becloud them from acknowledging, appreciating, celebrating, and preserving each other's values. That is, you should acknowledge whatever value your spouse has that is appreciated by outsiders. Your spouse's gifts, position (in office, church, or society), and achievements must be valued by you in order to have a successful and romantic marriage. For example, a man said if his wife builds a house, he will never live in it because it is a bad omen for their marriage. What if God gave his wife the power to make more wealth? A person who does not appreciate the contribution of his or her spouse will never appreciate bigger things.

Some Challenges of Marriage

As mentioned earlier, every marriage has its challenges. Some of these challenges are as follows.

1. **Finance.** Money managed improperly can be one of the greatest challenges facing marriages, apart from

sex and communication. Financial stress often leads to marital stress. Lack of money often distresses the woman and makes the man feel incapable of meeting the needs of the home. The answer to this is for the couple to pray and work harder for financial blessing for the home. The skill of financial management is another challenge. The answer to this is to let the couple talk about how the family money can be managed, and a budget should be made and followed. The couple should not value money more than their marriage. Couples are advised to be open-minded in order to acquire the financial management skills necessarily to support their home. Seminars and books on family finances are recommended.

2. **Communication.** Communication comes from the Latin word *communis,* which means "common" or "to share". When man communicates, he is trying to establish a degree of commonness with someone else. It can also be defined as the process by which information is passed between individuals and organizations, by means of previously agreed-upon symbols. A leading marriage counsellor says that at least half of all divorces result from a communication gap between spouses. It has equally been proved that women talk more than men. Women speak 25,000 words daily, whereas men speak 12,000 words daily. No wonder marriage is facing challenges! Women are looking for men whom they could talk to and who will listen. Talk about your pains, joys, success,

failures, and feelings. Never fear sharing with your spouse what is paining your heart.

Dr Shay Roop says, "A marriage that does not take time to communicate with words, voice tone and torch is a marriage headed over a cliff."

3. **Sex.** Sexual dissatisfaction has brought so much friction to marital relationships. Some have even ended in divorce or separation. Sexual compatibility is the key to good marital health because it reduces marital tension or marital unfaithfulness. Dr Humilton said, "To say that most marriage frictions does not find its source in sexual, maladjustment. At any rate, the frictions which arise from other difficulties would be ignored in many cases if sexual relationship was satisfactory." Thrive for sexual satisfaction by taking advantage of this book in your hand.

4. **Third-party relationship.** This has led to the breakdown of so many marriages. Wrong counselling from the enemies of your spouse and marriage could lead to marital problems.

   • Never make friend with an enemy of your spouse.
   • Never discuss your marital problems with someone who has no marital integrity.
   • Never discuss problems with a person who has no answers.
   • Discuss with your pastor and anyone who has the interests of your marriage at heart.

5. **Overdependency.** A person having dependency issues is like a half person. That half person finds another half person and believes that two halves will make a whole.

Signs of Dependency in a Relationship

- Initiating most of the calls and time spent together.
- Talking about the relationship more than the other person does.
- Feeling anxiety when not with the partner.
- Being angry when the partner wants to be alone or have time with friends.
- Being unwilling to voice disagreement with the partner's plans or feelings, for fear of rejection or disapproval
- Being unhappy when the other seems perfectly fine when you're not together.
- Wanting to know everything the other person does, thinks, and feels.
- Feeling indecisive and unable to make decisions without the other's reassurance; feeling crushed and devastated with the other's criticism.
- Carrying a disproportionate responsibility for the relationship.
- Feeling helpless and constantly needing reassurance for fear the relationship will end.

Dependent people have no borders between themselves and others. They look to others for approval and affirmation. Love your spouse, but let your spouse be himself or herself.

6. **Children.** Children are blessings from God, but their presence or absence in a marriage should not be allowed to destroy the peace and purpose of God for marriage.

   a. Training your children should be given serious priority. Children left on their own will bring shame. The spouses should come together and bring up their children in the fear of God. Never substitute the love for your wife or husband for the children. Never support the children against your spouse.

   b. The absence of children could dash family's and couple's expectations; it could pose great challenge to their ministry. The couple should encourage each other, fighting together without blaming each other. They should both depend on God just as other Bible patriarchs did.

Notes

_____

_____

_____

_____

_____

_____

_____

_____

_____

_____

Chapter 4

SEX IN MARRIAGE

Generally, sexual intercourse in a marriage can be practiced with presumptions or knowledge of how to engage in it. However, a common situation is the lack of knowledge of sexual intercourse even when already in a marriage. Lack of knowledge of sexual intercourse in marriage is understandably due to overwhelming moral consciousness and teachings surrounding sexual intercourse. Information that is available to married adults in society is usually distorted, perverted, immoral, and padded with a lot of anxiety and uncertainty. This is because parents, guardians, and experienced adults who ought to teach couples the art of sex in marriages fail in this responsibility. Therefore, a lot of mature youths getting ready for marriage have vague knowledge of this important subject.

> *Romance at this stage should be a combination of verbal expression and physical exploration.*

> *Foreplay should be before the act of sex and also can continue after the act of sex, when one of the spouses is not sexually satisfied.*

The take-off point of sexual relationships in most marriages is usually not predicated on any meaningful objective other than general knowledge of sexual enjoyment. The understanding is often that couples are expected to raise children as a result of their sexual relationship. This is a noble expectation in every marriage because God created sex for procreation or reproduction.

> *Sexual intercourse in marriage is both an art and an act. Sex in marriage is a composite of many things within a short period of time.*

However, the question is, is this the only purpose for which God created sex? Obviously the answer is no. There are other noble reasons for this God-given sexual exercise that are equally as noble as bearing children. These other noble reasons are where most couples lack knowledge. This chapter will focus on those areas in other to enhance knowledge about the sexual relationship in marriage.

Sexual intercourse in marriage is both an art and act. Sex in marriage is a composite of many things within a short period of time. This is the reason why many people concentrate on the later part of the art, than on the actual act of sex; they forget the preliminaries that are needed and constitute the longer part of sex. Casual sex with prostitutes and rape are classic examples of sex acts devoid of art. Often, these two unpleasant, ungodly sex acts take a short time and leave a lasting psychological scar. Sexual intercourse in marriage is not a casual affair; it involves some ingredients to facilitate romantic and sexual satisfaction.

Ingredients of Delightful Sex

The ingredients of sexual satisfaction in marriage are discussed below.

- **Preparation time.** Good quality time is to be earmark by the husband and wife to have romantic sexual intercourse. This time is to allow for the physical and emotional appreciation of one another. It could be time to shower (either individually or together) with the intention of getting ready for sexual intercourse. It could be time to assist a spouse in completing domestic chores, in order to save time for them to have sex. The most important aspect of this preparation time is to kick-start in the mind of the spouse the art of sex before the act itself. This stage adds value for sexual satisfaction, and it is an anticipatory stage for the sexual relationship which prepares the physiological reactions.

- **Romance.** Romance, according to Dictionary.com, means "To invent, or relate romances, indulge in fanciful or extravagant stories or day dream; to think or talk romantically; a romantic spirit, sentiment, emotion or desire". These meanings of romance should be understood and engaged in by the couple before sex takes place. It could mean expressing sexual prowess

> *Never rush your wife into sex, because it will only hurt her physically and emotionally. Gently guide her into sex through foreplay, and you will be surprised at the results you get.*

or desires. It could entail appreciating the physique of each spouse. Romance at this stage should be a combination of verbal expression and physical exploration (e.g., kisses, petting, massage, tight embrace, dancing to soft music).

• **Foreplay.** Prior to the act of sexual intercourse, couples must understand that psychological readiness does not automatically means their bodies are ready for sex. The romance stage will get the body and mind ready for sex. Foreplay directly targets the sensitive parts of the body and the sex organs of the body, to get them ready for sex.

This phase is completed, and couples are ready for sex when definite physical changes occur.

As the name suggests, it is playing with sexual organs or parts of the body that arouse the spouse before sex. Foreplay makes the couple sexually excited even if they have not thought about sex. Women require foreplay time which might be as short as five minutes. Without preparation time or romance, foreplay could be much longer if preparation was not done.

Foreplay could be before the act of sex and can continue after the act of sex, if one of the spouses is not sexually satisfied. Foreplay can continue after ejaculation and orgasm when the couple wants to continue with sex.

When this phase is completed and couples are ready for sex, definite physical changes occur.

- For the male, there is full erection of the penis.

- The vagina is lubricated, and the wife feels wet.

- Blood flow increases the size of labia and clitoris (which stands erect as would a penis).

- Blood pressure, heart rate, and respiration increase.

  The two most common and sensitive areas to touch in a woman are the clitoris and the breasts. Men can be aroused by sight, but most women are aroused by gentle touch. Never rush your wife into sex; it will only hurt her physically and emotionally. Gently guide her into sex through foreplay, and you will be surprised at the results you get. She could look forward to it next time.

- **Act of sexual intercourse.** Dictionary.com defines sexual intercourse as "genital contact, especially the insertion of penis into the vagina followed by orgasm; coitus; copulation". This quoted definition sums up in vivid terms what the act of sex means. Insertion of penis into vagina and copulation means tight body contact during the act of sexual intercourse. If there is only ejaculation, then sex is not complete – the man simply satisfied himself. The experience of sex was limited to the husband, and the wife wasn't involved in it other than as a physical object of stimulation for him. It should be an exciting, satisfying experience for both of them if the matters discussed earlier are fully considered before this stage.

At this stage of the sexual relationship, the degree of satisfaction of both of them lies exclusively in their hands. It is interesting to note that feedback of the wife's feelings at this stage communicates an ego massage to the husband that he has done a great work in addition to ejaculation.

We would like to add here that foreplay and the act of sexual intercourse can be greatly impaired by frigidity, which is now called hypogyneismus by therapists. This is a condition which is found in certain women. A woman may have a lack of sexual desire or may experience low libido; she refuses or avoids sexual intimacy, or she may endure it without being able to reach orgasm, finding little or no pleasure in the act. In other cases, a woman may have difficulty being aroused, or sex may cause considerable pain or discomfort. The root cause can be emotional or physical. Whatever the cause, frigidity can result in conflict and strain in even the most secure marriages.

There might be treatment options for frigidity depending on the underlying causes and symptoms. A communication problem is often a fault for lack of sexual desire, so try discussing your partner's feelings. If frigidity is due to emotional

> *The experience of sex should be an exciting, satisfying experience for both of them.*

problems, discuss it openly with a counsellor. If it is due to physical problem, it is recommended that a professional's help is sought; consult a gynaecologist, general practitioner, or health professional.

In the meantime, if the woman decides to go ahead with sexual intercourse just to satisfy her husband or to not starve her husband sexually before help comes their way, they can try using virgin coconut oil because it is easily absorbed in the body. The oil should be used to caress the vulva, clitoris, laps, breasts, and all sensitive areas of the woman's body during foreplay. There will be some lubrication of the vulva and vagina to ease penetration of the penis so that sex will not be too painful for the wife.

Let us quickly put in here that this coconut oil can be used by any couple in the art of sex to arouse the wife more, and she will likely look forward to sex the next time.

Notes

_____

_____

_____

_____

_____

_____

_____

_____

_____

_____

Chapter 5

TIPS TO ACHIEVE SEXUAL SATISFACTION

Maximum satisfaction for both husband and wife can be achieved if they consider some of the following tips.

Frank communication at this stage. The act of sex is designed for the wife to be at the receiving end, with innermost feeling of the act of penis insertion into her, so it is advisable for her to be active in communication at this stage. This will help the

> *This stage of penetration, the insertion of the penis into the vagina and thrusting, is the point where sexual satisfaction or dissatisfaction is established.*

> *These two forms of communication (verbal and bodily touch) make the difference between a woman being considered hot or cold in bed.*

husband regulate the speed, the rate, and the depth of penis insertion. It will help sustain and maximize their satisfaction. Passive responses from the wife at this stage may not be helpful. Romantic touches that are necessary for the husband to retain an erection (turgidity) will readily come to play. These two forms of communication (verbal and bodily touch) make the difference between a woman being considered hot or cold in bed. It is interesting to note that feedback of the wife's feelings at this stage communicates an ego massage to the husband that he has done great work. This is the point that makes sexual intercourse in marriage more delightful and satisfying than casual sex.

Orgasm is generally the peak of satisfaction for women. However, not all women get to this point of sexual satisfaction, due to either a knowledge gap or other factors that have been discussed in this book. Close to 100 per cent of men get sexual satisfaction at the point of ejaculation. This stage of penetration, the insertion of the penis into the vagina and thrusting, is the point where sexual satisfaction or dissatisfaction is established. Whatever level of satisfaction a husband and wife derive from a particular sexual experience, it is usually helpful after sexual intercourse for them to stay romantic and not sleep or jump out of bed, because the other may not be satisfied. Talking offers the couple an opportunity to lovingly appreciate and review their concluded sexual experience, and try to improve on it next time. This should not be a formal discussion, and it should not be done every time sex occurs – that would be mechanical – but the discussion should occur once in a while. It is important for the wife not to douche (flush the vagina) or run off to wash off as if sperm is a piece of dirt, because it is something that came out of the husband's body. Moreover, douching washes off normal organisms in the vagina, exposing her to infection, which consequently reduces bonding. Continuous douching will expose the woman to a high risk of infection.

- **Spice up your sexual intercourse experience.** It should be noted that sexual satisfaction can come from different postures, different styles, and even different locations within the house. Couples should try anything that they have not tried before. Moreover, it should be noted that sex during pregnancy is not a taboo, but during pregnancy the posture must change to give way to the bulging stomach. The missionary style (man on top of woman) is not the only posture for sexual intercourse. Try others to spice up your sexual experience. Make sure sex is fun, be dynamic, and do it in different places. This will make your love making interesting and fun. The more you both want to enjoy your lovemaking, the more you will want to have sex, and you will be closer to each other.

Naura Hayden says, "As long as two people stay sexually in love, they will never part."

More Tips to Achieve Sexual Satisfaction

It is good to note here that for desirable sexual satisfaction, both men and women should continuously cleanse their veins and arteries to have free flow of blood. If these vessels are clogged with heavy

> *Lack of a romantic sexual relationship in marriage impairs the bonding process and can give the spouse a sense of rejection.*

metals, excess calcium, and cholesterol, the circulation of blood is slowed throughout the bodies, including the sex organs.

When a man has erectile dysfunction, his obstructed penis blood vessels are unable to supply it with blood. This blood flow is essential for the penis to be hard and ready to penetrate his beloved. His penis should be engorged with blood to get big and give him and his wife enormous pleasure.

The same applies with a woman's clitoris, which is her "mini penis", and her nipples. They all need good blood circulation to be aroused, no matter the amount of foreplay (playing with her clitoris and sucking her nipples). If there is not enough blood supply to these parts of the body, she will never be aroused.

To cleanse your veins and arteries, we recommend you take organic supplements that have no after-use side effects. We take supplements from Forever Living products like Argi Plus, which helps removes cholesterol so that blood easily circulates to the brain and other parts of the body. Another supplement good for the heart to be able to pump blood effortlessly is CoQ10. This helps remove the fat accumulated on the heart wall, which impairs the heart from pumping blood and eventually makes the heart too stiff to pump, leading to many sicknesses and consequently death. You can get information from the Forever Living product website, or contact any of its business owners for details.

Some Facts about Sexuality between Men and Women

Men

- Men need appreciation and respect.

- Men are visually stimulated.

- Men want action.

- Men want sex more frequently.

- Men need less foreplay.

Women

- Women need to be valued by the husband's love and attention; love is time spent together.

- Women need to be tactically stimulated; sex begins with non-sexual affection.

- Women want a relationship.

- Most women want sex less frequently.

- Women need more foreplay.

Causes of Sexual Dissatisfaction

Sexual dissatisfaction has brought a lot of challenges to many marriages. It has banished peace, joy, and harmony from many homes. Sexual dissatisfaction

Broken-down trust is one of the most difficult vices to be mended.

is one of the causes of marital tension and unrest. When couples go for counselling, they are sometimes unaware that sex is the source of their problem, and they blame it on finances and other problems. The lack of finances in the home greatly affects the wife, but let's calls a spade a spade. When sex is the actual problem, stop beating about the bush.

Apart from asking for sex at the wrong time, environmental disturbances, non-conducive atmospheric conditions (e.g., excessive heat, drunkenness), here are some other causes.

> *Improve any kind of odour emanating from the body to enhance sexual satisfaction.*

- **Physical conditions.** Sexual dissatisfaction can arise because of sexually transmitted diseases, sickness, alcohol and drug addictions, thyroid problems, vascular diseases, diabetes, and medications that reduce desire and consequently cause poor performance in bed. Body odour and mouth odour gotten congenitally (born with it), or odour due to lack of proper hygiene, can repulse anybody who comes near. Spouses should seek advice on how to improve any kind of odour emanating from the body to enhance sexual satisfaction.

- **Psychological conditions.** Anxiety, fear (e.g., of unwanted pregnancy), fatigue, unresolved conflicts, harboured anger, stress, resentment, unmet personal needs, poor communication and growing apart, frigidity, and insecurity are causes of sexual dissatisfaction in marriage. If not properly handled, these factors could escalate to bigger marital problems.

- **Hormonal conditions.:** Men experience significant sexual changes as they age, and that is important for the wife to note. At a later stage of life, erection is difficult and may be delayed. He needs more sensual touch for the couple to have good sexual intercourse and be satisfied. For the woman during menopause, there is a drop in testosterone, and that reduces a woman's desire for sex, affects her arousal capacity, and makes orgasm more difficult. This means the husband has to go the extra mile in foreplay and sexual intercourse for her to have orgasm.

Notes

Chapter 6

THE CONSEQUENCES OF SEXUAL DISSATISFACTION

Romantic sexual intercourse that is satisfying to both husband and wife adds good value and flavour to family life. However, consequences of regular, prolonged sexual dissatisfaction could be disastrous in any given marriage. Some of the consequences that can shake the foundation of marriage are discussed below.

Sexual dissatisfaction is one of the causes of marital tension and unrest. When couples go for counselling, they are sometimes unaware that sex is the source of their problem and blame it on finances and other problems.

Mutual sense of rejection. As mentioned earlier in this book, sexual intercourse is a way of bonding. It is therefore conversely true that a lack of a romantic sexual relationship in the marriage impairs the

They will consciously or unconsciously seek another object or subject of affection. This object or subject may be human or inhuman.

bonding process and could give the spouse a sense of rejection.

Mutual strong suspicion of infidelity. The tendency for a husband and wife who rarely enjoy sex means either of them might be suspected of having extramarital affairs. This situation can be dangerous for the marriage relationship because it affects trust. If trust is lost on matters of sex, then trust on other issues might be difficult to establish. Broken-down trust is one of the most difficult parts of a relationship to mend. Friendship is easily reconnected, but there may be no trust again.

- **High temptation for sexual immorality.** As sexual beings, couples may seek alternative sexual satisfaction if they're dissatisfied sexually with each other. The level of temptation depends on their environment at work, school, or wherever they spend most of their time. There are a lot of sexually dissatisfied people who practice seduction, and couples must be careful not to fall for these temptations. Watch out for the verbal and body languages of those who can easily betray their intention to seduce.

  > *There are a lot of sexually dissatisfied people who practice seduction. Watch out for the verbal and body languages of those who can easily betray their intention to seduce.*

- **Mutual diversion of affection.** Due to a high sense of mutual rejection, there is a tendency for both husband and wife to seek attention elsewhere.

They will consciously or unconsciously seek another object or subject of affection; this object or subject may be human or inhuman. For instance, a sexually dissatisfied spouse may transfer his or her affection to pornography, sex novels, or sex movies and get addicted to that. This mutual diversion of affection may be so bad that a spouse may not care what his or her spouse does with another person sexually as long as the spouse leaves him or her alone. People also turn to drugs and drunkenness.

- **Psychological and emotional instability.** As earlier mentioned, sex is both psychological and emotional. Where there is sexual dissatisfaction in marriage, all these aspects are destabilized. Almost everything will go wrong in the temperament and psyche, and this situation can be horrifying. It will take a good sex therapist and marriage counsellor, as well as the help of the Holy Spirit, to trace the disorderly behaviour of a dissatisfied couple to a sex problem. For example, rapists are emotionally and psychologically disoriented, and that is why they get involved in sexual scandals that are unimaginable and unexplainable. The same goes for cases of people who indulge in incest, masturbation, and sex addiction through use of toys on themselves. This also goes for those who indulge in sex with animals. The booming global sex trade attests to the reality of huge number of sexually dissatisfied persons who patronize both male and female prostitutes. You may do well to recommend this book to your loved ones as a token of your love for their social well-being.

- **Transferred frustration on siblings and close relations.** The matter of sexual dissatisfaction in marriage has a ripple effect on children and close relations because of the emotional and psychologically disorientation. Behavioural patterns of sexually dissatisfied couples will unconsciously be transferred to close contacts. Visitors and friends to the home may not be spared from irritable behaviour towards them as a result of misplaced aggression.

- **Lack of bonding.** Bonding in marriage is usually facilitated between husband and wife by a romantic sexual relationship. When sex becomes dissatisfying in marriage, a major means of bonding in marriage is impeded. Although other activities could facilitate bonding, they may not be as effective as sexual intercourse, which covers the psychological, emotional, and physical spheres of a relationship. As sexual dissatisfaction grows deep and longer in marriage, bonding between husband and wife is harder. Bonding through sexual intercourse is inevitable for the success of a marriage.

- **Lower productivity at work.** When couples are sexually dissatisfied, productivity at work is likely to nose dive. This is because the couple's minds are likely to be preoccupied with options for meeting their sexual appetite. The time taken to explore these options will naturally encumber the time for the business, and when options are exploited, the transferred affection discussed earlier will require devotion of time, energy, and resources which ought to have helped the person's work. Clear examples are found in people who spend their hard-earned income on gifts and items to satisfy their extramarital affairs. Some who cannot afford it may take loans to make up for their extra spending. The low productivity at work may result in not using their time and money to improve themselves in training and courses that could earn a promotion. Financial resources that ought to have been committed to boosting a business or trade are now used for the extramarital affair. For example, some pay for overseas trip, buy electronics, rent houses for new bedmates instead of putting money into the business or improving themselves.

- **Failing marriage.** Where sexual dissatisfaction becomes a pattern, the couple keeps to themselves and don't express their affection for each another due to sexual dissatisfaction, which removes a sense of dependency or need for each other. The next behaviour is for couples to begin living their lives independent of each other but under the same roof, managing all other aspects (attending church and functions together) yet not being in a shared relationship, which is marriage itself. The climax of this terrible stage of marriage is for the couple preferring separate places of abode without divorce.

- **High tendency for physical separation.** When a failing marriage persists without any positive intervention, the couple may be tempted to feel that it is better to stay apart from one another. They believe because of their social standing, feelings for their children, and doctrines of their faith, they may want to leave independently and separately without changing their marital status. This is what some refer to as a marriage of convenience. The truth is that the marriage no longer exists. They may be convenient, but the marriage at this stage has collapsed and failed. Even though divorce is not being formalized, divorce is simply the burial of a dead marriage.

> *The marriage at this stage has collapsed and failed. Even though divorce is not being formalized, it is the burial of a dead marriage.*

- **Incest.** Incest is where family members have sex with each other. Fathers have sex with their daughters, mothers have sex with their sons, or children have sex with each other. Incest attracts the curse of God, and His punishment comes upon anyone who practices it. In times past, in order to preserve the tribe, religion, and language, incest was encouraged. Now the population is too high, although some cultures around the world still practice it.

Some causes of incest include the following.

i) Ignorance to the relationship between spouses. This is seen in most cities whereby two adults see each other, like each other, get pregnant, and begin to live together as couple, not getting to know each other's parents and relations. There's no visitation to each other's village to see if they are related.

ii) Cohabitation of a group of grown-up children of the opposite sex in an accommodation.

iii) Parental carelessness. Adult children should not be sleeping together with their sisters in one room or one bed. Parents should watch when siblings touch and get too close sexually with each other. Sometimes those involved like this don't want to get married to people outside the family.

iv) Demonic attributes and activities in the home, whereby people within the family have sex for money, for a ritual, or to attain an important position or gain power.

• **Lost vision, ministry, and calling.** Sexual dissatisfaction could make a minister lose his or her vision if it is not properly managed. Many of the opposite sex are out there, ready to open their arms as a result of their dissatisfaction. It now brings two dissatisfied persons together in the quest of searching for satisfaction.

• **Sexual perversion.** Pornography, homosexuality, and lesbianism could come into play as a result of a lack of sexual satisfaction. People turn to alternatives to satisfy sexual desires. Judah's second son, Onan, released his semen on the ground so that he would not produce offspring for his late brother. God considered what he did to be evil, so He put him to death (Gen. 38:8–10). What is the difference with what Onan did by pouring out his semen on the ground and masturbation? Masturbation brings Christians spiritually low, without the power of God, and eventually they backslide.

Notes

_____

_____

_____

_____

_____

_____

_____

_____

_____

_____

Chapter 7

LIVE MARITAL ISSUES DISCUSSED

We are including in this book issues of marital relationships that individuals usually come up with in live discussions during couples seminars, couples retreats, couples fellowship, couples workshops, premarital or general counselling, and Sunday schools. From experience, many couples do not know where to turn to with some of these questions. Most of them are either leaders in society or even in the church, and people look up to them. We wish to discuss these issues because most of our readers may find them helpful; "without guidance people fall but with many counselors there is deliverance" (Prov. 11:14, CSB).

Please note that names in this chapter are not real. However, the questions were compiled from real questions asked over the course of decades of our teaching and preaching around the world. The answers to questions asked are our personal opinion and are not exhaustive or sacrosanct.

Some Questions about Sex and Romance

Q1. John: *Since I married my wife fifteen years ago, she has never said or behaved liked she enjoyed sex. She will always say I am disturbing her, and if she agrees, she will lie there like a log. Anywhere I turn her, she remains there and will tell me to finish quickly so she can sleep. We have gone for counselling and discovered that her mum told her sex is only needed when she wants to be pregnant, because men break women's hearts. No matter the prayer and counselling sessions we attend, she has not stopped her behaviour. What do I do?*

John should make a frantic effort to seek more relevant counselling from a sex therapist. In our opinion, it will take some time for the wife to be completely healed of her indoctrination from her mother. In addition, we recommend resources of sexual matters (marriage seminars, books, tapes, etc.), which could speed up the healing process. You should not give up because her sexual drive could be ignited.

Q2. Maxwell: *I have been married to my wife for seven years now. There was a time we were separated but later reconciled. Now does not give into sex when I demand it, because she says I don't give her enough money for food. This has led me to demarcate the house into two to cut her off, so she could come back to me. Am I wrong, and how do I make her to perform her duty as a woman?*

To answer the question of whether he is right or wrong, Maxwell was wrong to expect his wife to come for sex or resume their sexual relations because of that demarcation – which will worsen the situation. It is not the best way to settle this conflict. It is commendable that Maxwell and his wife overcame the evil of separation. We advise them to discuss and identify the common interest of attraction that helped them to come together, and whatever they arrived as the common point of attraction should be developed and strengthened. A good sexual relationship is one of the methodologies to strengthen that attraction. We recall the words of Nauran Heyden: "As long as two people stay sexually in love, they will never depart." We recommend that Maxwell and his wife read Heyden's book *The Sexually Delicious Marriage.*

Now to the issue of "not enough money for food, due to no sex". She will not give into sex. For food to be available in the home, we advise Maxwell and his wife plan and work harder to provide for their home. In our opinion, money for food should be viewed separately, even though they are both important. Sexual denial is not a good means to press for the provision of food in the home. It is simply an additional problem to the existing lack of food in the home.

At this point, we will like to reiterate that sex should not be seen as a duty but a responsibility of both husband and wife.

Q3. Marie: *I found out my husband, Joel, had HIV without telling me before our marriage. I was tested positive when I went for antenatal screening. I hid it because I thought I'd brought it into our marriage, but when I could not hide it anymore, I told his brother. The brother told me Joel had HIV before we got married. Now I gave birth, and the baby died because I breastfed the*

baby against nurses' advice. I am afraid of sex because I despise my husband for what he has done to me, and I don't want a reoccurrence of pregnancy. How do I live with and have sex with a man who deceived me like that?

We sincerely sympathize with Marie for this traumatic experience. This is one of the realities of life. It is not the worst situation that could occur in a marital relationship. The HIV status of Joel affecting her could have been the other way round because she was not sure whether it was her or Joel that brought it into the marriage until Joel's brother confirmed it.

In other words, what if it was Marie who would had infected Joel? It is on this basis that reasoning and understanding should prevail. She should forgive and love Joel. In our candid opinion, in order to manage the rest of their lives together in love and fruitfulness, they must manage their health condition. There is no need to be afraid of pregnancy because they can still have babies unaffected by HIV, with proper medical supervision. We recommend they seek medical help before considering having babies. There are recent medical discoveries that show their health condition can be managed so that they have a fruitful union. By way of encouragement, we want them to know there are other health conditions that are worse than HIV, such as hepatitis, Ebola, hypo- or hypertension, and heart failure, which could kill silently. They should take their medication seriously, and they will live long by God's grace.

Q4. Jack: *You have talked about foreplay and romance. My wife seems to be disgusted by sex and says "Do it quickly and leave me alone." I am frustrated.*

Jack needs to know the cause of his wife not giving into sex. It is not impossible that his wife might even be more frustrated on the issue than he is. Jack may do well to discuss the issue first with his wife and then with a sex therapist, to determine what the problem is with his wife, with him, or even between the two of them. Now that he is frustrated, we advise him to immediately see a sex therapist to put an end to his frustration. He should try romance (holding hands, walking) not only when he has sex in mind, to prepare her mind for sex. Romance does not start in bed. He should get resources that they could read together to help their situation.

Q5. Mat: *This question might sound stupid, but I always wonder how men and women of seventy years and above have sex. They seem not to be strong enough to perform sex as young people would. Is there another way of getting satisfaction without exerting energy? You see them remarrying even at old ages.*

Because Mat's question is a funny one, our answer might also be funny. My wife and I are far away from being seventy or above. You will have to wait till you are seventy to experience it, but since you want to know, our suggestion is that you seek out elderly couples and research it. Ask them a few questions about how it is done – and you can share your findings with us too! But on the issue of strength needed for sex, we have discussed in this book that is not only physical strengths that is required for sexual satisfaction. Romance, communication on sex, and foreplay are things that do not require strength and yet are necessary before the act of sex. When those preambles are done properly, the act is easier and enjoyable without much stress. Aged couples spend most of their time together shopping, visiting friends, scrubbing each other's back, and fighting and reconciling. These are the things that can constitute romance, which makes sex easy.

Q6. Mercy: *I usually have blood flow for up to seven days after having sex with my husband, who is a pastor, and he will still request more sex. I suspect he is in the occult. What should I do?*

We want her to seek medical help and see a specialist (gynaecologist). If it is a spiritual problem, you should go for counselling from trusted servants of God and seek spiritual help. We advise her to go for counselling with an open mind, not suspecting her husband yet, so that she does not cloud her thinking until it is confirmed by God's servants. If the husband is in the occult and wants to be delivered, then the two of them will go for deliverance.

Q7. Nancy: Regarding **women** ***whose churches allow the men to marry two or more wives, what if these women are not satisfied sexually? Should these women get satisfaction outside marriage?***

Please note that a sexual relationship in marriage is the responsibility of the parties involved in it. It is not a duty, and therefore anyone who is involved in polygamy or polyandry will have to work out what is acceptable to ensure satisfaction of all persons involved in the relationship. In this case because there are more participants in sex, all who are involved should seek extra knowledge on how to get the best for all of them to be sexually satisfied. They should discuss it with their partners and seek solutions from a sex therapist.

This book focuses on how to help eliminate extramarital affairs in marriages as much as possible, so that couples enjoy their partners. Getting satisfaction outside marriage is *not* recommended.

Q8. James: *Money seems to be the problem of most marriages, as I see it. How do we tackle the problem of "no money, no sex"?*

James, please know that money and sex in marriage are very vital, but they are of different importance in the relationship. Money must not be a precondition for sex. The patronage of prostitutes and harlots worldwide is based on the principle of money for sex, and marriage is more than that.

Issues of money and sex in marriage should be treated as separate issues and must be treated on their own merits. Couples should work harder to make more money available for their families. James's wife should cope with reality that money is not all marriage is about.

Q9. Juliet: *What annoys me is that immediately my husband ejaculates, he sleeps – whether I am sexually satisfied or not. This has made me despise sex despite foreplay or anything else he does. What should I do?*

We advise Juliet to keep her sex drive and discuss the issue with her husband. She should seek counselling on how to help her husband last longer or get erect again after ejaculation. They should seek medical help if the problem persists, and they should seek more knowledge and resources on how to enjoy their sex life.

Q10. Lina: *I rarely have sex urges, and I always feel my husband is disturbing me after a long day. My husband is accusing me of having an extramarital affair because if not, why don't I ask for sex? Should I go into sex pretending to enjoy it? What is the way out?*

Lina, you need to tell your husband and convince him you are not having an affair. We advise you to not pretend you enjoy sex. Instead, create time for sex. Manage your time (put sex in time table), and avoid being over worked if possible. Sex is a natural thing and should be approached so that your marriage will not crash. Sex doesn't have to only be at night when you are tired. Early morning is good too, before you both go out. Weekends are also there to plan for sex.

Q11. Flora: *Regarding having frequent sex, is sex a food that you eat every day?*

Yes, sex nourishes the soul and the body, just like food does. Sex nourishes the body because physical exercise is involved. Just as food gives satisfaction to the general mechanisms of the body, so does a sexual relationship. Sexual appetites differ from person to person. Flora, her husband, and any other couple facing the same problem should find out the sexual appetite of each other and adjust to meet each other's needs. The issue of frequency of sex will be addressed, and they will adjust to accommodate each other's sex drives.

Q12. Philip: *My wife does not take her bath in the evening, and we live in a hot climate. Having sex is not enjoyable because the smell from her armpits disturbs me. She refuses to correct this behaviour. How do you advise her?*

Philip will need also to create another time for sex after she has taken her bath, like in the morning. We suggest he invites her for a bath when he is taking his bath, and if possible, he can provide a fan or air-conditioning to cool the room and reduce sweating. He could help her with some house chores to enable her a set time to take her bath before going to bed. If, after all these attempts, she does not change, then he should help her see a marriage counsellor.

Q13. Jerry and Maryanne: *We want to know how sex settles conflict in marriage.*

We will start with the story of Mr and Mrs Barry, who had a hot argument and did not talk to each other for days. When Mrs Barry wanted to break the silence, she tied a towel around her, knowing full well that when she bent to pick up anything, her backside would show. She bent to sweep the floor in front of her husband, knowing that they had been starved of sex for some days. Mr Barry straight away grabbed his wife and took her to their bedroom. This is an illustration of how sex can settle conflicts. When there is a quarrel and misunderstanding in marriage, the couple seems to fall apart, not wanting any bodily contact. Bodily contact and verbal communication are involved in sex and are a good route for reconciliation. A person may not give his or her body willingly if the person's mind is not into it – that could be called rape, if he or she is forced. By the time a spouse willingly gives into sex, it means that he or she wants to put things right and holds no more grudges.

Q14. Jeff: *My wife has no sex drive – or better put, she has low sex drive because she is never excited about sexual intercourse. We have been married for thirteen years. I have a problem with rare sex (sometimes once a month), but I think the problem is with the word of God, which forbids sex before marriage. I would have backed out of the relationship if I'd realized this before marriage. I have tried everything, but she has not changed, and we rarely have sex.*

We sympathize with Jeff because he has tried all he could. We still have to offer our suggestions. Seek more knowledge together with your wife. Counselling is needed from a sex therapist. Also, spiritual counselling is needed. Maybe the phobia is due to past experiences.

Jeff needs to also do a sincere self-examination as to whether he is the reason why she is put off. We use this opportunity to advise would-be couples to go for premarital counselling, where sex in marriage is also discussed, so that everyone knows his or her role in marriage to avoid an occurrence like this couple. The standard of God is no sex before marriage, and that cannot be changed. There's no "tasting" sex to discover if this is the right person before marriage. You have to continue to pray for your wife and your relationship.

Q15. *What are some of the most helpful resources on sexuality and marriage?*

Getting Your Sex Life off to a Great Start: A Guide for Engaged and Newlywed Couples, Clifford and Joyce Penner (Word, 1994)

"Intelligent, deliberate preparation for a lifetime of sexual pleasure is a worthy investment, and this book is an excellent guide to doing just that. Renowned sexual counselors and best-selling authors Cliff and Joyce Penner take you through an encouraging process that begins by dispelling sexual myths and then guides you in getting to know yourself and each other emotionally and physically. With reassuring enthusiasm and straight forward advice, the Penners show you how to clarify your expectations and pursue true marital passion through creative, step-by-step exercises and easy-to-understand examples."

The Gift of Sex: A Guide to Sexual Fulfillment, Clifford and Joyce Penner (Word, 1981)

"This is an ideal guide for understanding your own sexuality and the sexual relationship in marriage with all its pleasure, drive, frustration, and fulfillment. The book focuses on the physical dimension (how our bodies work), the total experience (having fun, pleasuring, stimulating, etc.), moving past sexual barriers (differing sexual needs), resolving technical difficulties (no arousal, pain, etc.), and finding help, all from a thoroughly Christian perspective built on the premise that sexuality is a gift from God. The Penners have included well over a dozen sexual enhancement exercises that have proven helpful to thousands of married couples. The book is readable, practical, frank, and intimate."

A Celebration of Sex: A Christian Couple's Manual, Douglas E. Rosenau (Thomas Nelson, 1994)

"This thorough book provides assistance on dozens of sexual issues and answers specific, often unasked questions about sexual topics. It presents all married couples with detailed techniques and behavioural skills for a full awareness and understanding of sexual pleasure. One of the strengths of this volume is the inclusion of several detailed diagrams and illustrations. The goal of *A Celebration of Sex* is to help you create the one-flesh union that God has ordained, the spiritual merger of wife and husband."

The Sexual Man, Archibald D. Hart (Word, 1994)

"This is an honest, carefully documented book that answers dozens of questions about today's men and their sexuality. Dr. Hart has surveyed more than six hundred men to discover what satisfies men sexually, what sexual fears and failures haunt them and the keys to a fulfilled and guilt-free sex life. This book, however, is not for men only. Every wife can learn more about her partner by reading these pages that are packed with helpful charts depicting male sexuality."

Your Wife Was Sexually Abused, John Courtright and Sid Rogers (Zondervan, 1994)

"If your wife has been sexually abused, this little book is a must. Written by two men who have had to deal with their own wives' past sexual abuse, this book will help you find healing amidst the pain and confusion. Each heart-moving chapter includes questions for thought and discussion that will help you work through your own personal situation to a healthy and stable marriage."

Note: Question 15 is culled from *Questions Couples Ask* by Dr Les Parrot III and Dr Leslie Parrot.

Notes

_____

_____

_____

_____

_____

_____

_____

_____

_____

_____

BIBLIOGRAPHY

Allgeier, Albert and Elizabeth Allgeier. *Sexual Interaction.* Lexington: DC Health and Co. (1995), 219.

Dictionary.com.

Fernandez, Henry. *Faith, Family, and Finances* (2012), 144.

Harly Jr, Willard F. *His Needs, Her Needs* (2013).

Hart, Archibad D., Catherine Webner Hart, and Debra L. Taylor. *Secrets of Eve.* Clashville: Word Publishing (1998), 197.

Hayden, Naura. *The Sexually Delicious Marriage* (2008).

Ladewing, Patricia, Marcia London, and Salty Olds' Essential Material, Newborn Nursing. Redwood City: Benjamin/Cummies (1994), 519.

McDowell, Josh D. "Is the Bible Sexually Oppressive?"

Parrot, Les and Leslie Parrot. *Questions Couples Ask* (1996).

Penner, Clifford and Joyce Penner. *Getting Your Sex Life off to a Great Start* (1994).

Reichman, Judith. *I'm Not in the Mood.* New York: Morrow (1981), 64.

Roop, Shay. *God's Design for Female Sexuality and Intimacy* (2004).

Roop, Shay. *God's Design for Male Sexuality and Intimacy* (2004).

Ziglar, Zig. *You Can Reach the Top* (1998).

Printed in the United States
By Bookmasters